What Would YOU Do?

Should Theo Say Thank You?

Being Respectful

Rebecca Rissman

LIBRARY

Chicago, Illinois

To contact Capstone Global Library please phone 800-747-4992, or visit
our website www.capstonepub.com

Edited by Daniel Nunn, Rebecca Rissman, and Siân Smith
Designed by Steve Mead
Picture research by Mica Brancic
Production by Alison Parsons
Originated by Capstone Global Library Ltd
Printed and bound in China by Leo Paper Products Ltd

16 15 14 13 12
10 9 8 7 6 5 4 3 2 1

Library of Congress Cataloging-in-Publication Data
Rissman, Rebecca.
 Should Theo say thank you? : being respectful / Rebecca Rissman.—1st
 ed. p. cm.—(What would you do?)
 Includes bibliographical references and index.
 ISBN 978-1-4329-7240-0 (hb)—ISBN 978-1-4329-7246-2 (pb) 1.
Decision making—Juvenile literature. I. Title.
 BF448.R57 2013
 395.1'22—dc23   2012017434

Acknowledgments
All photographs © Capstone Publishers (Karon Dubke).

Contents

Making Choices

We make choices every day, such as "Should I help carry the bags?"

Our choices have effects.

Ask yourself if your choices will have good or bad effects.

Should Theo Say Thank You?

Theo has been given a birthday present. Should Theo say thank you?

Theo could choose to say thank you.

Theo could choose not to say
thank you.

What Would YOU Have Done?

If Theo had said thank you, his friend would have felt good about giving Theo the present. If Theo had not said thank you, his friend might have thought that Theo was rude and Theo could have hurt his friend's feelings.

Should Henry Tell the Truth?

Henry lost his sister's toy.
Should Henry tell the truth?

Henry could choose to tell the truth.

Henry could choose to lie.

What Would YOU Have Done?

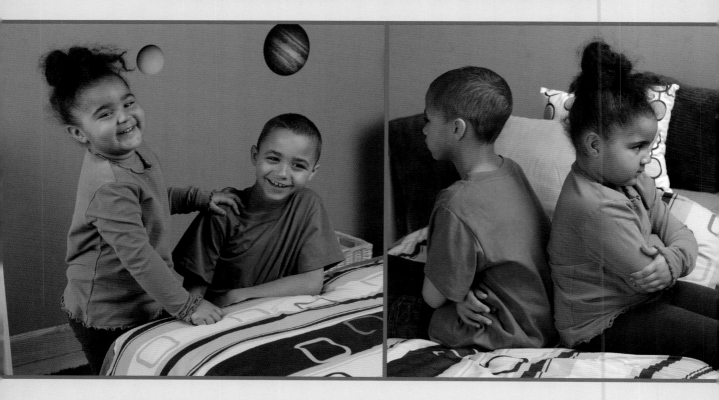

If Henry had told the truth, his sister could have understood, and they could have looked for the toy together. If Henry had lied, his sister might have been upset and decided not to lend him any more toys.

14

Should Bella Wait Her Turn?

There is a line to use the slide. Should Bella wait her turn?

Bella could choose to wait her turn.

Bella could choose to push in front of the others.

What Would YOU Have Done?

If Bella had waited her turn, she and the other children could have all used the slide. If Bella had not waited for her turn, she would have annoyed the children who were waiting. They might not have wanted to play with Bella again.

Should Charlotte Clean Her Room?

Charlotte's room is messy. Should Charlotte clean her room?

Charlotte could choose to clean her room.

Charlotte could choose not to clean her room.

What Would YOU Have Done?

If Charlotte had cleaned her room, it would have been easy for her to find her favorite toys. If Charlotte had not cleaned her room, she might have lost things or stepped on a toy and hurt herself.

Picture Glossary

choice a decision

effects the results of a decision or something you choose to do. Choices can have good or bad effects.

lie to say something that is not true

truth something that is real or correct

23

Index

Notes for Parents and Teachers
Before reading

Explain to children that our decisions have consequences, or outcomes. Consequences can be good or bad. Making good decisions can result in good outcomes. Draw a decision tree on the board for the children to see. At the top, write a question, such as *Should Theo say thank you?* Underneath, write *yes* and *no*. Then encourage children to brainstorm the outcomes for each decision. Record their answers underneath the *yes* or *no* on the decision tree.

After reading

Help children to make their own decision trees. Ask each child to write down a scenario and the possible decisions. Then, encourage them to think of as many outcomes as possible and record them. Have children circle the best decision and discuss it together.